Nene's Prose

Ancel Mondia

Ukiyoto Publishing

All global publishing rights are held by

Ukiyoto Publishing

Published in 2022

Content Copyright © Ancel Mondia

ISBN 9789360162962

*All rights reserved.
No part of this publication may be reproduced,
transmitted, or stored in a retrieval system, in any
form by any means, electronic, mechanical,
photocopying, recording or otherwise, without the
prior permission of the publisher.*

The moral rights of the authors have been asserted.

*This book is sold subject to the condition that it shall
not by way of trade or otherwise, be lent, resold,
hired out or otherwise circulated, without the
publisher's prior consent, in any form of binding or
cover other than that in which it is published.*

www.ukiyoto.com

Contents

P. O. W. E. R. (September 10, 2021)	1
L. I. V. E. (September 28, 2021)	4
Isms (October 22, 2021)	8
SCAR (November 15, 2021)	11
Insecurities (December 8, 2021)	14
Toxicity (January 7, 2022)	17
Illuminating and Ultimate Gray (January 31, 2022)	21
Beauty (February 23, 2022)	24
Fallacies (March 23, 2022)	27
Life Lessons (May 13, 2022)	30
Protect the Earth, Protect Our Lives (June 24, 2022)	34
Versus (July 27, 2022)	38
About the Author	42

P. O. W. E. R.

(September 10, 2021)

I wish to be kinder, wiser, and braver on my 27th birthday, which came on the 2nd day of September.

In a few words, I wish to be empowered. I don't want to be manipulated by a fast-paced life, so I try to find a balance between living in the moment and securing the future. I seek to convert tragedy to wisdom and irony to insight, so I opt to stay positive despite the real-life drama.

I want to be driven by passion and purpose that result in productivity, so I decide to remain mindfully true to my heart. I aim to understand human nature, so I make sure that I give equal attention to reason and emotion. I choose to acknowledge, accept, and adore my unique self, so I act on regulating my space and boundaries.

My wish to have power over myself, my life, and my future results in my discovery of power as an acronym for patience, optimism, will, empathy, and respect.

Patience

I have realized that power lies in a virtue named patience. My pace isn't based on the influence of time. I have to savor each moment of my existence as well as work for my future independence. I can learn to grow from every experience if I uphold character and excellence.

Optimism

I have discovered that being in power is embracing positivity by breathing wisdom through a tragedy and living with intuitive insights in the face of life's ironies. Optimism turns out to be my good quality when it's seen in my humanity because lifting spirits mirrors my great abilities.

Will

I have believed that my power is my free will, especially when it's paired with my passionate skill and my purposeful action to fulfill. My life can carry on with thrill when I don't have secrets to spill and pain to kill.

Empathy

I have agreed that to live in power I have to master my emotions. As I govern my life with reason and affection, I have to show empathy in human relations, too. To be kind isn't only my option because to be of heartfelt service is my mission. That's the only way I can have satisfaction.

Respect

I have known that to manifest power I have to develop respect by protecting my boundaries and ruling my space while connecting with others. It's myself that I have to project and my life that I have to direct as my heart and mind reflect my reality.

As I turn twenty-seven, I also wish for contentment, acceptance, and growth. I don't want to live in unhealthy life comparisons, unfounded beauty standards, and nonsensical primitive thoughts.

I hope that my birthday is another beginning of abundance and merriment in my life as I remain grateful for the gift of life given to me by the benevolent God that is the sign of both love and power.

L. I. V. E.

(September 28, 2021)

Earlier this month, the world observed World Suicide Prevention Week (September 5-11). I wish to share the life lessons I have learned from a very special person in my life. I have known her as an individual filled with courage and ambition who has unexpectedly been reinforced by a devastating psychotic episode.

Diagnosed as having schizoaffective disorder, she has undergone mental health treatment for years. Schizoaffective disorder has symptoms of both schizophrenia and mood disorders. Schizophrenia includes delusions, hallucinations, disorganized speech such as frequent derailment or incoherence, grossly disorganized or catatonic behavior, and negative symptoms such as diminished emotional expression or avolition.

Mood disorders, sometimes called affective disorders, make up an important category of psychiatric illness consisting of depressive disorder, bipolar disorder, and other disorders.

The disorder may also be a distinct third type of psychosis. Psychosis is a mental disorder in which the thoughts, affective response, ability to recognize reality, and ability to communicate and relate to others are sufficiently impaired to interfere grossly with the capacity to deal with reality.

Schizoaffective disorder has the diagnostic criteria of either a manic or a depressive episode. Mania is a mood state characterized by elation, agitation, hyperactivity, hypersexuality, and accelerated thinking and speaking. Depression is a mental state characterized by feelings of sadness, loneliness, despair, low self-esteem, and self-reproach.

The disorder also includes delusions or hallucinations but the cause is unknown. Delusion is a false belief based on incorrect inference about external reality. Hallucination is a false sensory perception occurring in the absence of any relevant external stimulation of the sensory modality involved.

Mood stabilizers alone or with antipsychotic agents are important in the treatment. Psychosocial treatment includes family therapy, social skills training, and cognitive rehabilitation. The information comes from the eleventh edition of Kaplan & Sadock's "Synopsis of Psychiatry".

Living with her illness, my friend has persistently combatted nervous breakdown that inflicts fear-inducing and self-negating perceptions. She has almost surrendered in her psychological battle, which appears to be a never-ending process. But her mind impressively remains to be her greatest asset.

Her lingering thoughts have switched from death to life, so she has constantly chosen to live over taking her life. She has realized that to LIVE is to love and lead, instill and inspire, value and voice, and evolve and embody.

To love and lead

She opts to live, which means to push no one and to plead for nothing. She learns to appreciate her gifts from above, which she utilizes to bring meaning to her existence. By loving and leading her own life, she continues to be alive.

To instill and inspire

Because she knows that she has the entire lifetime to fill with her aspirations, she prefers to live. She believes that her will is her way towards the triumphs that she deserves. She lives by instilling in her heart the desire to inspire.

To value and voice

She chooses to live by consciously saving the essence of her existence. While everything continues, she rejoices in the idea of staying alive. By valuing her spirit and voicing her mind, she knows she has to get on with her life.

To evolve and embody

Because she believes in the concept that she is somebody, she accepts the life she has to live. She embraces the depth and complexity of tuning into her spirit and body. She learns to live by evolving and embodying the life within her.

Her life, including her struggles, is far from over. But her fortitude and brainpower have become her permanent trademark. She asserts that taking one's own life is never the answer, so she voluntarily surrenders to the Supreme Being.

She believes that she can gladly give her all to free herself from everything that ties her to earthly existence because she is done vying for worldly things.

She has loved and led her life, and together we have instilled and inspired life. She has valued her life, and together we have evolved and embodied life. She is a very special person to me as we are one. She is me and I am her.

The moment for death shall eventually come to me, but I hope to make sure that I have fully and truly lived.

Isms

(October 22, 2021)

Prejudice has made your world contaminated. As your views change from utopian to dystopian, your world changes from being beautiful to being ugly.

Discrimination has made their world crooked. As their outlooks change from idealistic to cynical, their world changes from being pleasant to being unpleasant.

Stigma has made my world corrupted. As my beliefs change from spiritual to secular, my world changes from being peaceful to being hostile.

Our world, which has become all about superiority and inferiority, has changed drastically by five isms: racism, classism, sexism, ageism, ableism.

1. Racism divides our world by race, which means the color of our skins, the size of our bodies, the features of our faces, the condition of our countries, and the origin of our blood.

2. Classism divides our world by class, which means the amount of our money, the price of our food, the

number of our properties, the availability of our resources, and the status of our economies.

3. Sexism divides our world by sex, which means the type of our organs, the force of our physicality, the function of our systems, the nature of our behaviors, and the way of our thinking.

4. Ageism divides our world by age, which means the duration of our lives, the freshness of our selves, the energy of our actions, the naivety of our judgments, and the level of our maturities.

5. Ableism divides our world by ability, which means the perfection of our health, the activeness of our senses, the normalcy of our parts, the saneness of our minds, and the degree of our capacities.

Where superiority and inferiority prevail, comes the persistence of inequality that points to the realization of your dystopian views, their cynical outlooks, and my secular beliefs.

On the contrary, if we would change our world, we should change the five isms to five equalities: race equality, class equality, sex equality, age equality, ability equality. Or else we shall end up in regret as we let our world label us.

1. Our world may label us deformed, which means ugly, unfortunate, and cursed; but we can be beautiful, fortunate, and blessed.

2. Our world may label us poor, which means uneducated, abusive, and slothful; but we can be educated, temperate, and industrious.

3. Our world may label us feminine, which means domesticated, submissive, and melodramatic; but we can be masterful, assertive, and rational.

4. Our world may label us ostracized, which means odd, insecure, and lost; but we can be normal, confident, and self-aware.

5. Our world may label us psychotic, which means insane, ridiculous, and useless; but we can be sane, praiseworthy, and useful.

If we do not want to have regret as an utterance, a feeling, and a consequence, we should invalidate the labels fabricated by the five isms. You should debunk the misconceptions that have formed into prejudice.

They should negate the fallacies that have developed into discrimination. We should dispel the myths that have turned into stigma. We should know that we can either change or regret.

SCAR

(November 15, 2021)

I have grown with a scar that represents my terrible beauty and my silent screams. I have lived a life that is controlled chaos consisting of bittersweet experiences.

The clock was about to strike midnight and the rain was heavily pouring down. A group of people in a hospital rejoiced for having a new addition to the family. Their tears of joy, however, turned into tears of pain when they beheld me.

They anticipated to see a fearfully and wonderfully made baby, but I was born with a cleft lip and palate. They perceived my life as a precious gift but my birth defects as misfortunes.

Months later, my parents alleviated my misery by scheduling surgeries for me. My congenital splits were replaced by a scar, which was ridiculed by other children my age. Random people considered me defective as they underestimated my power of speech. I was bullied, mocked, and humiliated because of my ugly physical appearance.

I was too ashamed of my existence and I silently learned to express myself through writing. I, surprisingly, discovered my love for the English language and literature as it deeply taught me to be proud of my deformed image.

Though my speech faltered, I excelled in the field of language. Though I was doubted for my communication skills, I turned into a master of English. I have become the person I am today because of my SCAR, which for me stands for sympathy, contentment, authenticity, resilience.

Sympathy

Because of my scar, I have understood the common feelings of humanity. I have learned that we must share positive views that build and support one another. I have known how to relate with others and appreciate the life lessons that shape them. Because I can see the value of every being, I keep the nurturing relationships I have with them.

Contentment

I have deeply experienced both happiness and gratitude because of my scar. I have preferred and accepted a simple yet peaceful life. I have learned that wanting to be somebody else, more, or better is of no use. It is a good mindset and not a perfect image that guarantees bliss because what we feel is more important than what we see.

Authenticity

Because of my scar, I have embraced and taken pride in my individuality. I have known that nobody can falsify my own truth without my consent. I have been willing to comfortably present my genuineness to the world and even the universe. I have been unpretentiously standing with the belief that I need no one to validate my reality.

Resilience

I have become tough because of my scar, which constantly reminds me that I am strong enough to combat and recover from any pain. I have realized that every single thing for me is not yet over. I also have learned not to hide in misery and fears. I have shamelessly faced the challenges that can, unexpectedly, help me become better.

I was born with a cleft lip and palate but I am not cursed or an accident. I am beautifully put together and everything in my life falls into place. My scar is the imperishable source of the matchless beauty and inimitable wonder in me.

Insecurities

(December 8, 2021)

Being in my twenties, I have realized that I must live my life on my own terms and pace. Adulthood, as people say, is all about ideals, romance, and stability. However, in my case, it is different.

I have learned to be accepting, content, and courageous. Various people expect me to be physically attractive, to be in a relationship, and to be secure in life. Nevertheless, I am not the person they have anticipated me to be.

I have heard their unfavorable feedback on me, and my insecurities have begun to build up. I know the feelings tend to break me, so I have repeatedly converted them into ideas that make me. I have listed my top three insecurities which I think almost everyone my age can relate to. I also have written my ideas which I hope will lift and enlighten others.

1. Non-ideal Body

I have been through different body types, from rectangle to hourglass to round. However, I do not ever let my shape make me think of myself less of a woman. I stay confident in my own skin and weight.

Through the inconsistency of the physique, I have understood how temporal earthly forms are. Skin-deep beauty is never the basis of my worth as a human being. I am more than my skin. I am a wonderful creation whose beauty lies in my growth. It is not what is seen, the physical body, that matters. It is the unseen, the person within.

2. Single Status

I have experienced heartbreaks caused by romantic crushes that disappear and mutual understandings that end. I have never officially had a boyfriend, so I can surely say that I have been single since birth.

Despite the truth that I have never been taken, I do not ever think that I lack something in myself. I am whole, and nobody can make me feel half. I am not missing a part of me just because it seems that I will be a spinster. I am complete, whether my civil status will change or not. I am loved by no other than myself as self-love is the greatest love of all.

3. Unstable Job

I have felt shame for being incapable of keeping a stable job. I have resigned to take other opportunities where I can be happy. I have landed different jobs where I have not lasted long because they are not mentally healthy for me.

I am being scolded and criticized for living in the moment instead of securing a future. Nevertheless, I still do not want to settle for less. I firmly believe that the best is yet to come and great things are in store for me. I will continue to take risks to live life to the fullest. I will live rather than survive.

I do not allow my insecurities to intimidate and devastate me, so they have made me dauntless and invincible. I have conquered my greatest enemy, which is myself. I hope others will conquer themselves, too, and be dauntless and invincible as well.

Toxicity

(January 7, 2022)

"What makes you leave a job?" my interviewer queried.

In one single word, I mindfully replied, "toxicity."

Toxicity is a destructive quality, which primarily affects personal, social and professional aspects of existence. It annihilates self-image, relationships and work environment. Toxic people have unhealthy notions about themselves, so they get involved in mentally harming others, and they eventually make suffocating employment systems.

In a book titled Toxic People: Decontaminate Difficult People at Work Without Using Weapons or Duct Tape authored by Marsha Petrie Sue, six types of toxic people are identified: Steamrollers, Zipper Lips, Backstabbers, Know-It-Alls, Needy Weenies, Whine and Cheesers.

Steamrollers are known as exploders, dominators, tyrants, dictators, bullies, autocrats, oppressors, persecutors, or tormentors. They are not much fun to be around.

Zipper Lips are known as clams, tight lips, cautious thinkers, madly mysterious individuals, or verbal anorexics. By failing to contribute, they become a drag on any work group.

Backstabbers are referred to as psychopaths or snakes in suits. They have little conscience or ability to develop one. Their only goals seem to be power and personal gain.

Know-It-Alls are called content experts, authorities, and the "always right." They speak well and make you believe what they are saying, when in fact they could be leading you astray.

Needy Weenies are agonizers, worrywarts, wimps, vacillators, anxious Annies, and martyrs. They will drive you nuts and make you crazy with their neediness.

Whine and Cheesers are referred to as whiners, bad apples, complainers, faultfinders, naysayers, maybe people, and losers. They drain energy out of projects and people.

Toxic people are poisonous and hazardous members of communities consisting of diverse personalities that are supposed to share common goals. They stand against the idea and act of upholding humanity and supporting harmony.

Toxic people do exist so the human resources department, whose main function is recruiting the right people, must be a humane group of individuals. However, based on my own work experiences, I can assert that the HR department of many institutions ironically lacks humanity.

They must genuinely care about the well-being of employees to create and maintain a work culture of openness and growth. On the contrary, they are the toxic and distant people who aggravate and perpetuate career issues. They must be reminded that they fundamentally are the protectors of the employees' needs.

The HR must improve career paths to avoid stagnation. They must guide employees to stay in the company for a long time. They must provide additional training, educational assistance and management guidance. They must ensure the flexibility of the work schedule as they check the health and function of employees. The HR must remember that employees are people whom they must help in various life circumstances.

Nevertheless, the department can only fulfill their responsibilities by first fighting and defeating the toxicity within and among themselves. They are a resource for human beings, so above everything else, they must be the exponents of humanity. The human resources department is not given its name for no reason.

As I believe toxicity is caused by insecurity that worsens by envy, the individuals who make up the department must be of secure and humane personalities. The betterment of an entire institution comes along with the improvement of its HR.

Illuminating and Ultimate Gray (January 31, 2022)

The bright, cheerful and warming PANTONE 13-0647 (Illuminating), which reflected solar power, and the solid, dependable, and firm PANTONE 17-5104 (Ultimate Gray), which signified pebbles on the beach, were the two independent colors of 2021.

Their superb union emphasized the unwavering support that comes from different elements, such as optimism and fortitude. The two qualities that were greatly tested and definitely strengthened within me during the past year.

My 2021 was a wild mixture of contradictory events as it brought me both tears and smiles. It provided me with various experiences and gifted me with valuable insights. The authentic process of learning has been determined by randomness and filled me with surprises. However, the opposite emotions generated by the year also shaped a happier and stronger version of my distinct spirit.

Death is not an end

In 2021, my uncle and grandmother passed away. I used to get irrationally sad and absurdly afraid when I went to wakes and burials. But I began to see death in a different light. I have become grateful and happy for them as their painful earthly battles have ended. When they visited me in my dreams, I was assured that they were in a much better place now.

My childish mourning over the vague idea of death was replaced by a profound relief over the uplifting notion of everlasting life.

Connecting with others

Also last year, in the middle of a seemingly endless pandemic, I found the resolve to start a charitable project. I gladly held an online poetry event, which accepted donations of face masks that I excitedly distributed within my own community. It may seem a simple thing, but it gave me more realizations than one might see.

I felt more connected to my fellow human beings and found more purpose in my own precious existence.

I also willingly had my Covid-19 vaccination to help fight the global health crisis. I certainly believe that responsibly observing health protocols is an act of love, care, and protection for self and others.

Slowly going back to normal

Despite the seemingly never-ending threats of stagnation and despair, I feel fortunate that I was able to find the strength to thrive through difficult times. One of my great achievements was finishing my hard-earned master's degree that culminated in a momentous virtual graduation meticulously conducted by my beloved university.

Then, as the world has been gradually trying to bring back normalcy, I was unexpectedly given the chance to rejuvenate my spirit by traveling, for the first time ever, to the popular islands in my province. And before the eventful year came to a close, I was handed a new beginning by being gratefully employed again.

The significance of the beautiful pair of colors of 2021 mysteriously stirred my entire being. They precisely represented the unpredictable story of my cherished life during the complex year.

As 2022 embraces us, with its color PANTONE 17-393 Very Peri, may the fresh year be filled with inventiveness and creativity, hope and strength, and most especially, optimism and fortitude.

May an immediate future of both happiness and warmth bring the living world an empowering sense of newness.

Beauty

(February 23, 2022)

Mirror, mirror on the wall, who's the fairest of them all?

This classic line from the fairy tale "Snow White" mirrors the depth of humankind's desire to possess beauty. Beauty has been a common theme of stories from time immemorial until here and now.

As literature reflects real feelings and thoughts of real people, I know that Queen Grimhilde is living among us. We can become cold and cruel due to the obsession and envy that she represents.

Beauty has been associated with models, celebrities, and royalties; however, as the world has reached the present era, the concept of beauty has evolved and conjures different meanings for every person.

It is beautiful to know that there is beauty in everyone. Nevertheless, humans as we are, we have an ugly side that gets the better of us. We have lived in comparisons and being the lesser ones results in negativities that we choose to normalize.

I admit that I am also fond of the idea of beauty. I have been a victim of unfounded and unrealistic beauty standards. However, when I have experienced a seemingly spiritual awakening, I am able to put the puzzle pieces of trickery into place and see the whole picture of reality. I believe it is wisdom that I behold, so I want to share the newfound lessons that I have learned from what people label as beauty.

1. People know that our body eventually decomposes; it is inevitable. People know that external beauty decays and it is inescapable. However, they value one another based on physical appearances and attributes. People rely their worth on transitoriness or ephemerality of beauty.

Nevertheless, it helps when people begin to believe that beauty does not only belong to the youth. Life is a process and beauty is its cycle. Attractiveness or beauteousness does not equate to youthfulness. Beauty is the four seasons of life, it is not only the transitory or ephemeral springtime of existence.

2. Some people assert that the meaning of beauty is pleasingness and tidiness. Some people opine that the definition of beauty is freshness and flawlessness. However, people in general think that foreignness or atypicality is the quality that constitutes beauty. A beautiful visage is perceived as the foreign or atypical visage.

Nevertheless, it helps when people begin to understand that being beautiful is not being superiorly different from others. Being beautiful is being a segment of diversity.

Beauty is not different, it is diverse. Beauty is made up of people, it is not possessed only by some. It is not just the foreign or atypical, it is also the native and typical.

3. Beauty is bleached and people term it emptiness. Beauty is stained and people name it worldliness. People define multiform beauty as superficiality and wickedness. However, the changing loveliness among people is an attempt of one another to materialize the notion of fixed loveliness that they continue to invent.

Nevertheless, it helps when people begin to know that beauty is an innate quality of humankind. People can experiment with their looks as long as they stay aware that surface beauty cannot replace the beauty within. The exterior can only complement the character inside. Beauty is nature, which people can only nurture.

I hope that we shall stop asking a mystical object known as the Magic Mirror to validate what we consider as beauty. Let us recognize the reality that being beautiful is being natural, diverse and alive.

We are the world, the universe, and beauty.

Fallacies

(March 23, 2022)

I have undergone three crazy stages in life: childhood, adolescence, and adulthood. And as I reach the lingering (present) phase of my precious existence, I also realized that I've been long exposed to three wicked fallacies.

In the book titled, "Logically Fallacious" written by Bo Bennett, they're mentioned and defined as Appeal to Authority, Appeal to Common Belief, and Appeal to Emotion.

Appeal to Authority is referred to as using authority as evidence in an argument when the authority is not really an authority on the facts relevant to the argument.

Appeal to Common Belief is explained as when a claim that most or many people in general, or of a particular group, accepts as true, it is presented as evidence for the claim.

Appeal to Emotion is described as the general category of many fallacies that use emotion in place of reason in an attempt to win the argument.

I have certainly recognized the deceitful reality wherein the logical fallacies strongly attempt to crookedly shape my perspectives and obnoxiously mold my character. However, I'm being steadfastly saved and have become determined through balancing intuition and reason. I'm able to quickly identify and prevent logical fallacies from manipulating and misleading me.

In general, the logical fallacies generate and perpetuate vicious beliefs that severely annihilate their firm believers. The pretentious false authority, the lazy thinking society, and the irrationally fickle emotions forcibly push individuals to repeatedly engage in destructive deeds and normally commit harmful activities.

Because of logical fallacies, for instance, individuals develop the vice of drinking and smoking. They defend the hazardous actions because they witness the adults drink and the community smoke. When they do the same, they feel a sense of belonging.

Because of logical fallacies, individuals grow the habit of cursing and gossiping. They tolerate offensive actions because they witness the adults cursing and the community gossip. When they do the same, they feel a sense of connection.

However, when individuals choose the powerful intuition and mighty reason over wicked logical fallacies, they shall know that hazardous, offensive, and secular actions may only lead them to self-destruction. They shall begin to believe that they should have built, evolved, and loved themselves.

The self is the apparent evidence of the pure and sacred gift of life, so I wish individuals to nurture, protect, and value themselves. We should trust in our powerful intuition and reason. We should turn away from common beliefs or claims that don't necessarily reflect what is true. We should go beyond emotions and recognize logic and truths, but without losing our ability to feel and empathize.

With all the noise in the world, it can be hard to protect life's purity. Sometimes, the best course of action is to go with the flow instead of going against the tide.

But an undying hope remains, I want to remind everyone that today is the time to positively change and better ourselves. We're much stronger and far greater than the logical fallacies.

Life Lessons
(May 13, 2022)

I am a living thing made up of the diverse yet interconnected aspects of life. I exist in the general idea of both binary and inclusivity. I may only have one voice but I can speak for the many.

I live in the universe and the universe lives in me. I am both different from and similar to anyone else. I come from life and life comes from me. I belong to humanity who is both the giver and the receiver of life lessons. So I am sharing four of the lessons with everyone.

Balance your intelligence and attitude

What is intelligence without attitude? What is attitude without intelligence?

If you are smart but aren't nice, you tend to be cruel because you take things in an intellectual manner. You easily sense if you're being fooled, so you, being blinded by excess reason, quickly demonstrate self-entitlement.

Meanwhile, if you are nice but aren't smart, you tend to be tolerant because you take things in an emotional manner. You easily conform if you're being manipulated, so you, being blinded by excess passion, quickly exhibit self-pity.

One must not exist without the other because it only results in extremes. You must have both intelligence and attitude. You must know when to use your head and when to use your heart without totally silencing the one if the other speaks more.

You must learn balance as intelligence and attitude must be together.

Learn through your problem

We think that the problem is only the thing itself. We do not notice that the problem may affect other things connected with it. It plainly means that problems must not be cast away immediately. We have to deal with them, or else, they shall create larger problems. They must undergo the procedure of repair. It may mean the loss of other good things, but the benefit shall still be worth the sacrifice.

After the loss, bad things shall turn good. Along with them shall be the goodness of the whole. Life shall not be all about gaining, but about weighing and choosing. You shall pluck out problems, suffer their bigger damages, while cherishing the untouched good things within them; or you shall turn right what is wrong, pluck out the good things that hinder the repair, and attain the goodness of the whole.

Make the right way your way

When you are in time of prosperity, sharing your fortune with others makes you noble. Helping them spreads goodness that shows that you are a person of goodwill. However, despite all the kindness that you demonstrate, you cannot guarantee that you can never be wronged by others.

You can be betrayed and hurt but they're a reason to change, to be unkind particularly to yourself. If you wrong others simply because they have wronged you first, you downgrade yourself. If you rationalize that your wrongdoing is right simply because it is the means to get what you want, you become ignoble. When you act on ill will, it shows that you are a shallow person who cannot firmly stand for what is right and good.

When you are at this point in your life, you are astray and must find the right way back to the reparation of your life. If you have not still found your way out of the dilemma that you have created, you must not be wise in your own eyes and teach others.

You must not advise them to believe you and to be like you even though you think that your intention is good, because an astray person like you cannot guide others. You can only betray, hurt, and misguide them.

Live as spiritual being above everything else

I believe that we must not just exist and survive, we must learn and live. We are given a period of time to hold the gift of life and as recipients, we have the choice to utilize it based on its purpose or to misuse it due to our own will.

Life is not just the duration of being alive, life is the depth of being spiritual. We can be victimized by external circumstances, but we own the power to regulate our internal experiences. The meaning of life is produced by our spiritual growth, as above anything else, we are spiritual beings.

We can philosophize that we are just human beings that must follow our wants, but before the time of our lives runs out, we must realize that we are living souls that ought to fulfill our life's purposes. Life is not just our physical acts, life is our spiritual deeds.

These four life lessons that I have imparted with everyone are the things that I have personally learned from my existence. As we are uniquely related to one another, I hope that we continue to learn from ourselves and others. The things that determine life are no other than its lessons.

Protect the Earth, Protect Our Lives

(June 24, 2022)

Let's open our hands and let the raindrops fall on our palms. Let's relive the memories that render the generosity of the Earth.

The Earth is the provider of our physical needs, the sustainer of our mental needs, and the supplier of our spiritual needs. She has a natural beauty and a (sometimes) surreal quality. Schools of fish are found in her crystalline waters. Dozens of bird species thrive in her verdant jungles.

However, let's also compare the raindrops to teardrops of the Earth. Her sadness has been caused by the annihilation of her beauty. The Earth is asking for love, care, and attention from us, but we abuse, destroy, and ignore her instead. Amidst her striking and supreme comeliness, she has been suffering from worsening strain and deformation.

Let's come to our senses and repair our relationship with the Earth. Let's apologize to her by renewing ourselves and reciprocating her benevolence. She needs our five crucial actions: Evaluate, Aid, Recreate, Treasure, and Heal.

Evaluate

We must evaluate our consumption and effectively manage solid wastes.

Improper disposal has been affecting wildlife and biodiversity. Waste problems are contaminating ground, air, and water. Mismanagement of waste has led to exposure to toxins and spread of diseases.

We must adopt practices such as recycling and segregation. We must use environmentally-friendly materials. Proper solid waste management gives wildlife species the chance to enjoy their natural habitat.

Aid

We must give aid to the Earth to successfully combat biodiversity loss.

Decline of biodiversity has been caused by the loss of hectares of old-growth forests. The decline has been threatening plant and animal species, which are already endangered. The loss is worsened by the rise of illegal wildlife trade.

We must act as advocates of wildlife protection by reporting illegal trade activities. We must report those that maltreat plant and animal species to the right government agencies. Supporting the endeavors and initiatives of the environmental organizations must become our mission.

Recreate

We must recreate the Earth to solve air contamination.

Air pollution has been disrupting the natural flow of ecosystems. We must address the contamination by using cleaner fuel. We must reduce open burning activities, which make the air we breathe poisonous.

We must cooperate with one another as inhabitants of the planet. We must participate in relevant programs in managing the changing environment and apply our acquired knowledge to protect our surroundings for many years to come.

Treasure

We must treasure the Earth to successfully stop water pollution.

Water contamination has been killing lives since the mismanagement of hazardous plastics and chemicals.

We must address pollution by avoiding waste disposal in bodies of water. We must discontinue the dangerous dynamite fishing activities.

We must diligently work for environmental protection and responsibly take care of our natural water resources.

Heal

We must heal the Earth to effectively beat climate change.

The crisis has been causing extreme El Nino and severe tropical cyclones that endanger agriculture and food security. Climate change has been causing the spread of new, more deadly diseases. The impact also affects the marine ecosystems.

We must address climate change to stop species from leaving their natural habitat and migrating to harsh environments. We must reduce our carbon footprint by utilizing energy-efficient devices and appliances. Promoting eco-friendly businesses must be our objective.

Let's raise our fingers to the clear skies as the raindrops stop from falling. Let's anticipate the appearance of a rainbow and behold the restoration of the Earth's beauty. Let's be the Earth's warriors and protectors today.

Versus

(July 27, 2022)

The day after the election, I posted about my disappointment about the results. A professor-director left me seemingly wise yet subtly fallacious comments.

She opined that one should not judge another just because the circumstance turned out unfavorable. She added that the choice each one made had been selfish and nobody really had been thinking of another. My initial and lasting reaction towards her comments was indignation.

I was not thinking for myself when I expressed my political views, it was the nation I had in mind. I posted my outlooks with discernment and not with emotions.

After intuitively studying her comments, I got more disappointed to discover that even the mindset of an academic had remained selfish and shallow. She remained human in the subliminal derogatory sense of the word.

On the other hand, I continue to believe that we can be superhumans, which covertly had been at our core. We had been supposed to be social, intellectual, and spiritual — the aspects we had been made up of. We should not surrender to the downgrading conditioning or degrading programming that we had been experiencing.

We ought to speak, stand, and fight for change.

To be social over selfish

In the sad reality where the idea of respect is used as a method of manipulation, let us embody our own truth. Let us break the destructive familial pattern and end the vicious cycle. Let us free ourselves to be spiritually designed by the all-powerful cosmos.

We should not mistake selfishness for conscience, emotionalism for wisdom, and tolerance for love. It is all a lie, the belief that we ought to serve anyone we think we owe. We should think deeper than the corrupt, abusive, deceitful, and stagnant individuals.

It goes against humanity to deem ourselves exclusively in their possession.

We are not of anyone else but our selves. We deserve more than the limiting system and oppressive culture. We should decide not for fortune nor privilege but for fairness and inclusivity.

To be intellectual over shallow

Let us not normalize selfishness by tolerating shallowness, which equates to wickedness. We should not be deceived by those who pretend to perceive the whole picture. We should not be misled by those who conclude without knowing the stories behind.

Let us avoid making our judgment clouded. Let us prevent our perception from being blinded. We should not be astray. Let us not tolerate sportsmanship, which they demonstrate at its finest that leads to normalizing of being nonchalantly inhumane at its worst.

The juvenile and marginalized are not supposed to be silenced. We should utilize critical thinking particularly in critical times. We should apply analytical skills to determine even the external circumstances.

To be spiritual over sinful

We should defeat the culprits though they are the figures of authority, teaching, and influence. The government body that is known for service should not be composed of the self-serving. The education sector that is known for leadership should not be made up of the misleading. The media industry that is known for information should not be misinformed.

We should be aware that the culprits are part of systems that affect not only themselves but also others. They benefit at the expense of others. We should consider the use and claim of power. While the culprits use power for abuse, we ought to claim power for protection.

We should understand that willful mindlessness is destructive. We should be mindful that an individual cannot make a movement alone. Together we ought to combat for right and good. We should own our sense of self and purpose. We know we are not doomed yet.

As we resolve to remain fighting the good fight, we should know that our battles are not yet over. They should not come to an end as long as we have not yet come out victorious.

About the Author

Ancel Mondia

It was the second day of September, in the year 1994, when she was born to Anastacio and Cecilia Mondia.

She was a fourth grader at Oton Central Elementary School when her poem was published in the school newsletter.

When she studied at Oton National High School, she entered Special Program for the Arts.
She selected Bachelor of Arts in English as her degree and graduated cum laude at West Visayas State University. She finished Master of Arts in English and Literature at the same university.
To be a veteran writer is the dream she remains unwilling to surrender.

www.ingramcontent.com/pod-product-compliance
Lightning Source LLC
LaVergne TN
LVHW041557070526
838199LV00046B/2020